For Becki

When the Lord sovereignly designed
all things in eternity past, out of all the ages
He could have chosen, and out of all of the people
He could have ordained,
He elected you, in this life, to be mine.

Only God would've planned it that way!

God's Easter Promise

Only God Would Have Planned It That Way

Written by Todd Barsness   Illustrated by Shelly Hehenberger

CONCORDIA PUBLISHING HOUSE · SAINT LOUIS

If I would've planned out the Lord's Passion Week,

The throngs would be gathered and autographs they'd seek.

But the fickle-ish crowds would become a mad fray—

You see, only God would've planned it that way!

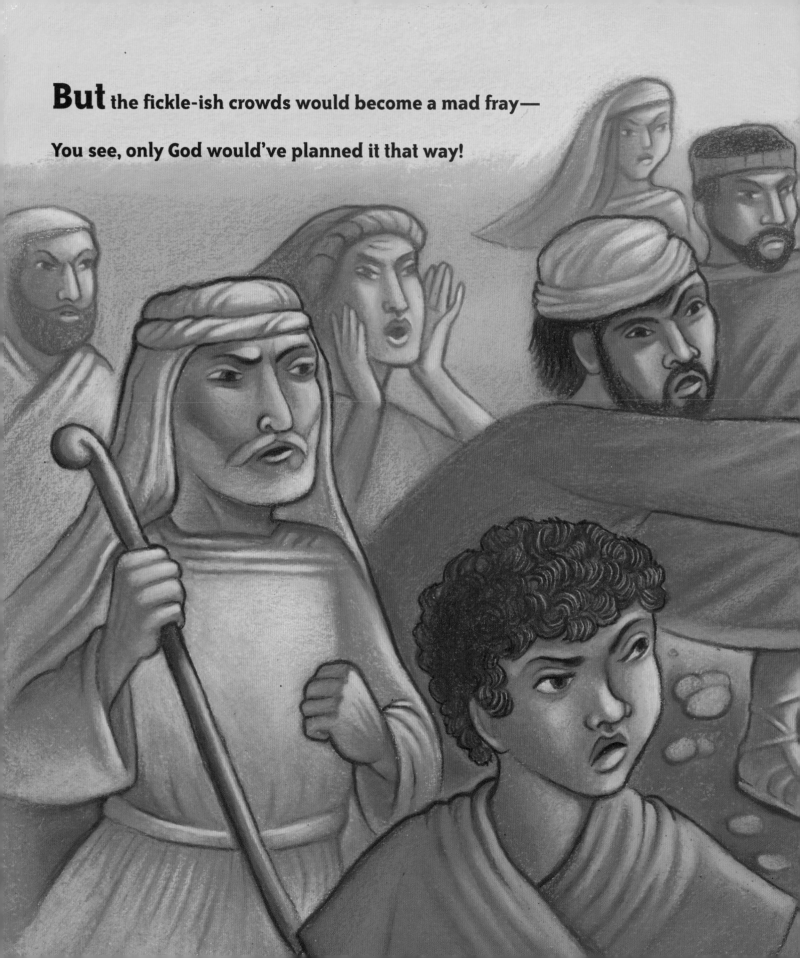

If I would've planned how a conqueror would ride,
I'd saddle a stallion with a big haughty stride.

Yet He hopped upon a small colt that spring day—

You see, only God would've planned it that way!

If I would've planned the last meal that He'd eat,

The best food and guests would be placed at His feet.

Yet Christ donned a towel and a meek servant's tray—

You see, only God would've planned it that way!

If I would've planned how He'd spend His last night,
I'd have thrown Him a party to bring Him delight.

But He wept alone; in great sorrow He prayed—

You see, only God would've planned it that way!

If I would've planned how a great king should die,

He'd have a grand funeral and thousands would cry.

But He hung on a cross on a day dark and gray—

You see, only God would've planned it that way!

If I would've planned the last statement He'd make,
I'd bring in reporters and notes they would take.

But "It is finished!" were the last words He'd say—
You see, only God would've planned it that way!

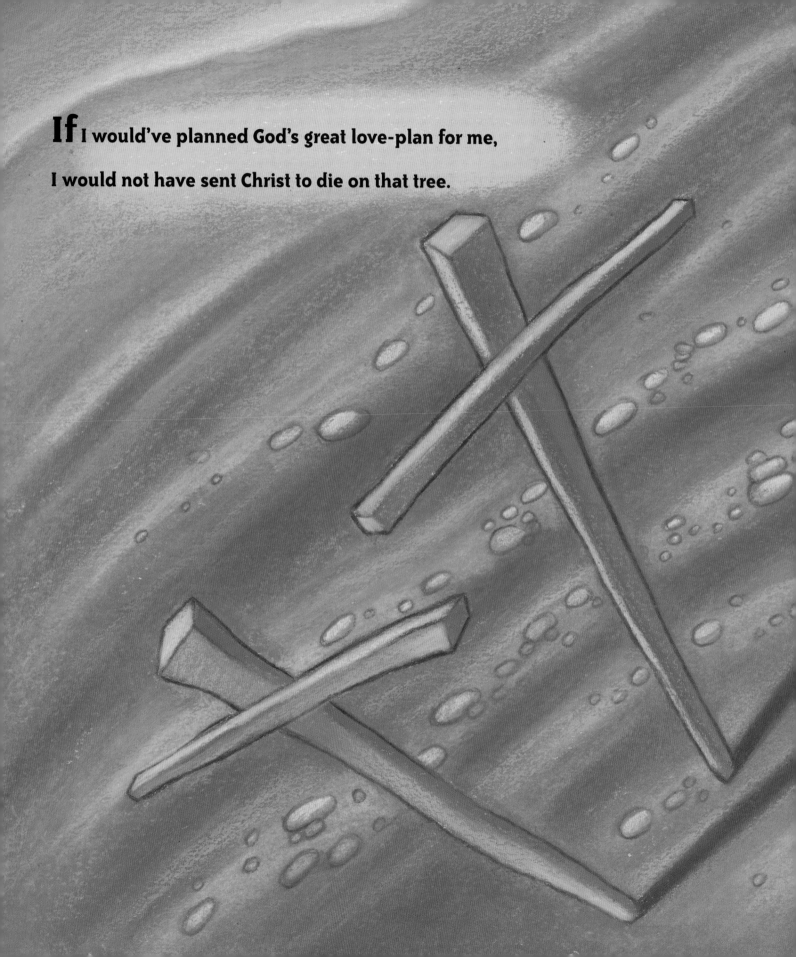

If I would've planned God's great love-plan for me,

I would not have sent Christ to die on that tree.

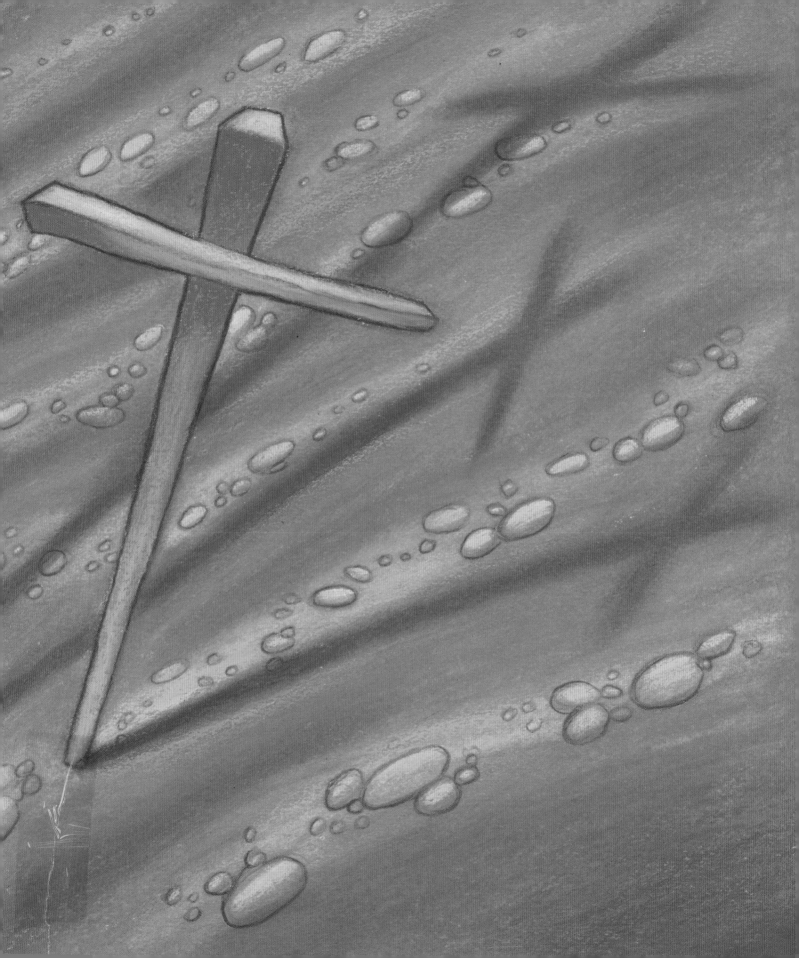

But God knew my sin needed infinite pay—

You see, only God would've planned it that way!

If I would've planned how Messiah would save,

He would not spend three days closed up in the grave.

But Christ rose from death that victorious day—

You see, only God would've planned it that way!

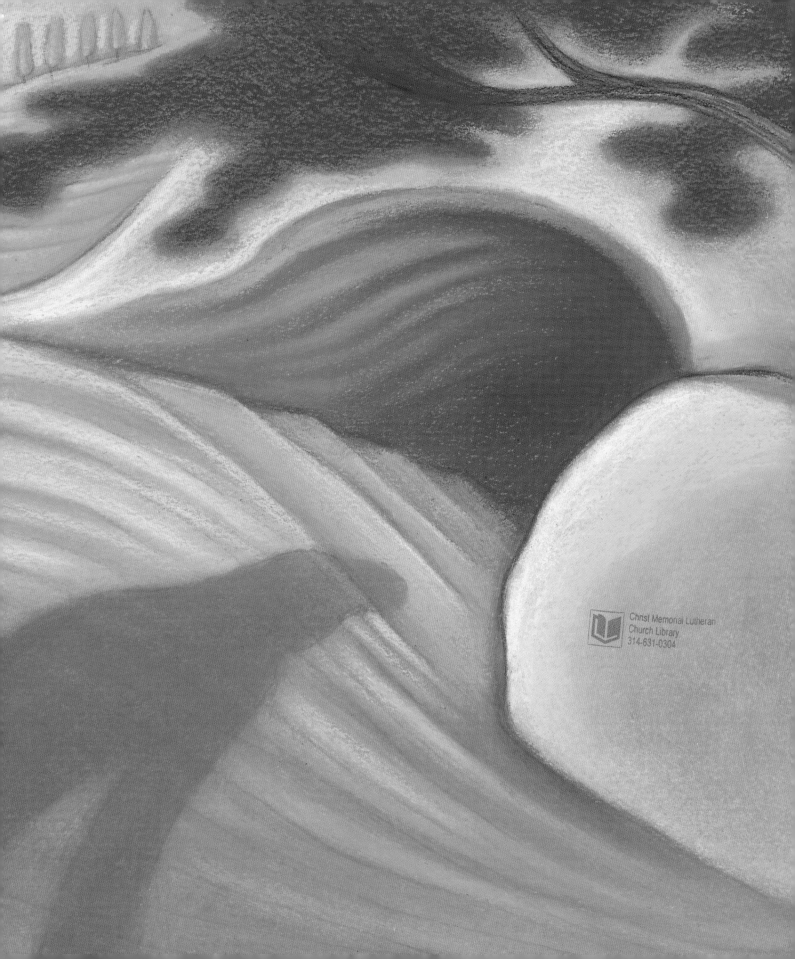

This edition published in 2006 by Concordia Publishing House
3558 S. Jefferson Avenue, St. Louis, MO 63118-3968
1-800-325-3040 • www.cph.org

Text copyright © 2002 Todd Barsness
Illustrations copyright © 2002 Concordia Publishing House

All rights reserved. No part of this publication may be reproduced, stored in a retrieval system,
or transmitted, in any form or by any means, electronic, mechanical, photocopying, recording,
or otherwise, without the prior written permission of Concordia Publishing House.

Manufactured in China

2 3 4 5 6 7 8 9 10   11 10 09 08 07 06 05